From Pearl Harbor Day to FDR's Birthday

7 December 1981—30 January 1982

Poems by

Jackson Mac Low

Sun & Moon Press
College Park, Maryland

First edition

ISBN: 0-940650-18-5 (cloth edition)

ISBN: 0-940650-19-3 (paper edition)

Library of Congress Catalog Card Number: 82-61709

Grateful acknowledgement is made to the editors and publishers of the following journals in which poems from this collection first appeared: *Conjunctions, Tamarisk,* and *This.*

cover design by Douglas Messerli

Sun & Moon Contemporary Literature Series Number 14

Sun & Moon Press
4330 Hartwick Road
College Park, Maryland 20740

for Anne Tardos

Contents

Hereford Bosons

1

Whether spoons being
not from accumulation institution
outside rim-shot castings
font of particular knickknacks

Dishes teach biases clocks
turned or torn peach pit tags
seeking flatter unctions
in secret territorial asps

Flags satisfy folly curtains
followers denaturings bracket
as tintypes or ferret traps
portulacas clack finically

Final cousins consummate
uproarious clawings pontoons
particularize foundation teams
or neatness callously essential

7 December 1981
New York

Hereford Bosons

2

Essential teams dream spoon accumulation
recent dryings factor
sacraments or spun potential wheels
glistering charismatic panel chlorine

Flaxen congratulation sweeps are
phonetic diatoms in choice tonic or
patent liaisons fortunate Dorchester
staffing panzer story quorums

Choruses descend fantasy casts
synecdoche notarizes loophole wreaths
fundamental tiger corps
limn in penetrable antres

Coral pornographies tangle plasters
panting hacksaw reverberation twists
trellised seasonal intent slot tears
an orchestra crenellates indignant

7 December 1981
New York

Hereford Bosons

3

Indignant Tonkin slush flask cars
react in zori fenestration
past unlikable forces porches
lenticular East Coast daisies particularize

Baseless enclitic bank pandering
orders faultless territorials
validity sprinkles encrusted Capri
tonally opalescent or geared

Gagged in allegation tingles
fan reality fractures
quarks perhaps or penis tesseracts
though panels clasp inspiration bones

Notary phantom clones imbibe
a zero angstrom pinking tie
mercenary panzer patch clues fling
on rough or clock torn Zinzendorfers

7-8 December 1981
New York

Hereford Bosons

4

Zinzendorfers ink at attaché sweeps
instant purulence calibrates
on banned Laputa pasteurization quills
Cleveland zinc clamps panic

Picnic infamy glazes sweet torques
tame palustrians thimble
whether geese in zigzag clank tumors
feature clandestine fonts or swank

Torn glance or fox timbers
clean ornate ingenuity Zunians
exaggerate and haggle on in
jar fortress pine strobes

Silence in coal faction clouds
entreats a pedal eloquence
sofa parka banner glimpse nodes
question in farcical steel realization

8 December 1981
New York

Hereford Bosons

5

Realization climbs a berried pit-a-pat
team peregrinations swive dotty
while suave tonsures tourniquet flakes
infallible tinctures glove

Craven coruscation drovers
deal gelatinous kinship crinolines
tierce inequality tangles or inks
when wheat zori flank pearl sprinkles

Tonal grasp chokers grow encaptioned
awaiting snappers crapulous tension
blank spots green in orphan pores
as Sweelincky benefaction dawdles

Claustral terrorism barracks craze
incipient banister phagocyte dreams
encysted Christmas practice cranks
lean dramatization panjandrums

8 December 1981
New York

Hereford Bosons

6

Panjandrums in galeate cramp zones linked
green sacrament factors lion wheels
distributing palpitant cholorphyll
zymogenesis of inert gradations

Orchestral classification timbrels
fantasize charismatic portrait quorums
Detroit calabashes answer derisive
as pasture brain curls thimble fractions

Fascination encapsulates flag-fair quartz
a Christian singularizes tinkling
regular existential barn sweep cleavers
greet evanescent wiper paradises

Sentence aggression channel proppers
dot iridescent gallimaufry grunts
zeal gleaners clink ambitiously
since pringling giants deracinate storks

8 December 1981
New York

Hereford Bosons

7

Storks creep or clap blank pilaster crowns
a tangling hatred scores in trust
a cluster of grim pine-swoggling flares
enriches amid kindred sycophant dawns

Glozing haunt-specific casuist pairs
predicate zoological distortion filters
zones of triumph-preventive pleasure necks
dissect a galley of glass Dionysian clinks

Rinks of roistering tunnel-sapient flanks
distend rebordering solfège banner swains
banking on portulaca finance test-tube pavings
in grassy sulfur-nasty solstice gear

Years of clinical finicking loophole corps
exaggerate hustings cube fenders
reverberation pillages blanks intensity
desultorily integrates in final stations

8 December 1981
New York

Wall Rev

A line is a crack
is an entrace furrow
distracting between thighs

Attracting between sighs
a parallel cataclysm
cannot tell its name

Active well of flame
tense entrance clues
obligate avoidance

8 December 1981
New York

Inkling Allegretti

1

Raised saying the myth of classroom
greeds the night pages topgallant raids
steadily assuming cloud wallopers peach
closed crinological tirades toaster trials

Isles of ill abundant kleptic teamwork
shirk dutiful aspidistra panic quotes
quaint rangers wrench engines diabolism strokes
as teacup tintinnabulation ferries quarter rolls

Holes in background maternal porridge clip
piss flickers where enclitic sirens veer
Klimtic pelicans endeavor servant peculations
so pained endocrine climbers rim beeswax shoetrees

Royal cordwainer calculators tenebrate shelving
near clear sulfuric poontang goose pimple sorts
drastic febrillation squirter hallway jerks
janissarialize tender tanks and strophe crumbs

Close the mountain lest the creepers clout
within the spoons are pickerels toads without

24 December 1981
New York

Inkling Allegretti

2

Without a clock dim teammates flail recursion
inertia withers whenever charisma divagates
divine improvements countersink helical proofs
pumps petulate or chorus nine sweet forests

Fearless kid green lavender sortilege tear marks
punctuate poinsettia salivation crackdowns
coasting dome splitters grip essential crystals
Isaiah driven hogs frustra corroborate

Clay immensity torments diamond felt cream
dreamers succinctly nuzzle spiting flag machines
maturation clusters macho chlorine pickers
sic cranberry tortoises melted saffron nerves

Curves in swerving pelts or gradual lynxes
link quincunxes where swearing stops filtration
narration clambers narrower porthole buckles
when pen sophistication limbers trimmers

Try more than kinship crust pollution toppers
lust cares to stretch or energize tense rompers

24 December 1981
New York

Inkling Allegretti

3

Rompers crystallize slim situation terminals
feral penthouse gluepots normalize rogant
toreador togas swell pacific hangout friezes
creased tearoom paddles propagate swinish

Syrupy tenderloins crow amid portly cleavers
nested sentence fences Gabrielize soonest
neuter tune perpetuators pileate seeker dust
severe pack dermatitis swill picklers wrinkle

Tinkling columns shift trim category grill mops
parched epistemological tories vitiate
quick declinable caster cleansers sort out
croziers nosological pilgrims pacify thickly

Swinking parish ink galumphers parrot Pan
as technical hideouts rust Canarsie krillworks
sostenuto daybreak hearses lurking flag
phylactery monuments pellagra measures

Mean so closely radiant benchmarks cluster
enraged piñata fur stripes leisurely bluster

24 December 1981
New York

Inkling Allegretti

4

Bluster seems or clinching models glowworms
pin tricked criminal rinsemongers fluctuate trigly
enriched or bestial clavichords nervously track
black history pun strokes tinsel flinchers crackle

Tackling cyanide pore hinges sample flints
distinct ambrosia hinters link completely
effete calliope crackdown glimpses torrefy
sorbic hosiers soap ensalmons glibly

Cryptic pill insisters lift enskied teak
whistle founders calisthenics withers
wintry peregrinations cast cerulean partisans
Paleolithically fitting part-time gimcracks

Lacking fibrous ornaments gabardine whey lakes
stake saturation plum turtles hurtle flailing
storm envisioners penetrate clamping stile folds
eroded cloakhangers ridge with viscid fractures

Fragment leeways tetanus swipers calculate
enraged centurion pickers force pumps lamely flagellate

24 December 1981
New York

Inkling Allegretti

5

Flagellate or curve sarcastic bubbles
trouble hovers backwardly over trusting
gusty clientele wrackers tenebrous fists
fiduciary crimson gift markers saturate

Obdurate hose soakers cloak encircled squids
secreting feldspar Rin Tin Tin entrapped
phynancial hectoring tests encysted irises
Falernian package heisters greet eupeptically

Rude euthanasia clues no stranded prankster
prancing fragmentarily listed Tuesday
root encyclicals grip inflated powders
pink helices indoctrinate enclosures

Roses strow Spode strategems spang handily
as crinkling filters glyphs terrestrial focuses
silky clinking glitters near fen tensions
Cyrenaic crannies clasp as gladiators

Tatter flagging tension hormones crisply
lips twist to fit phantasmic partridges wispily

24 December 1981
New York

19

Inkling Allegretti

6

Wispily catenas anchor tree stumps
encrusted grunting peristalsis flutters
forensic butter bleeds entreated Falstaffs
bland Pernambucan atrophy enables

Palaces of witless micturation clicks
sit or fling particular banshee phrases
Pelasgian cricket whippers falsify pintles
grim tenebration stalkers trim inconsistently

Nonexistent weather poppers chromatize wheezes
easy agricultural stripers traumatize
size fantasists encapsule eager wheat pearls
Delius fly stains disinter axiologically

Angry furniture blends belated guard strips
bistred package granters clip insistently
swift Eleatic fritterings snap benignly
beneath eared exponential disposability

Bolt grove tone panic slip driver infestations
eclamptic enamel cracklers sink gyrations

24 December 1981
New York

Inkling Allegretti

7

Gyrations whittle sticky mortuary pinpricks
fickle district cursive night growers banish
punished plunges function esoterically
enraptured bilious tricksters flash heroically

Lymph branding clysters prink irrational vintners
entrenching civilizing ink filled boulders
enfolded socialization gropers synchronize
exact Azazel educators rapid axioms

Rapt fraction taxers sack inconstant answers
sexualization benchers rend incompletely
seeded sweetmeat gill muff turners crunches
lurch hurtfully in astral stratification sweats

Fencing pterodactyls plump for socket ticklers
tickets lance or cobblers green simplistically
engardened weed eons deepen periphrastic lasts
cranky panacea students glue imprudently

Fools swung casual clippers toes or praised
bandanna gleamers Clytemnestra raised

24 December 1981
New York

Baltimore Porches

1

Crocodile pill Hecubas grin in fictive treats
diseased ensleekments cranny tyrannically zed
Arachne's ticker tape tatters steal gaunt sleeves
Toronto chorus skaters malignantly please

Bees' hoboes generate speedy factual digits
in turgid criticaster modal mugwump planes
pellucid strewn together streetcar pintos
arise in Eastern asteroidal lyrics

Pyrrhic veterans fuse or soothe a Samurai twist
till liquid crimping petals pattern data troves
thick nerveless loaves ecstatically excavate
filled fructuary useless Santa Claus wristmates

Fake dinosaur libations actualize intimate tens
torn fogey Gloucester peach trees glister clippedly
as sinkholes' operative district tuna tubes fixate

Quick credible tension cyclers satisfy turf modes
or mules' encaustic risible tinder clenchers
accosted seeker models idolize sleekly

24 December 1981
New York

Baltimore Porches

2

Sleekly hebetudinous ringers sink zinc visions
ritzy criminal trombones note in coated cracks
slack tinctures azure as ectodermal fill-ins
enfilade inválid patrician subunits

Unique invited ampere changers aggravate
enchained embossed derision stroking heat
effete enclosures roast infernal tourmalines
detective effort closers rinse in secret

Teardrop feature solvers gleam amid mud irons
tolling botulism crown designers dance among
sincerely hung potatoes glow as gloaters anticipate
evening skull teams' pantisocratic trances

Lancers curtly nodule instant Hebrides salts
exalted tall funicular troop cattle slippers
catalyze in aspirin filmic distance mixtures

Misanthropic mercantile fanicful ring zones
in zestful clamors leap in grievous valleys
ink and fiddlers' markups immensely sensitize

24 December 1981
New York

23

Baltimore Porches

3

Sensitize or creak in leap year lyrics
Illyrian canceled zebras swat or clot
in either crapulation ignorant z-strings
ennoble hopeless popish diamond finders

Climbers christen pediatric ramp nodes
insistent principality miners reify
defiant sickly sun crisp validations
denature zero Cratylus aping spinsters

Disfingered particle renters hint at telethons
enforced infractions riot against in clinics
slim critical Nesselrode totals pleasure polka dots
in giddy postulates braceleted clerics accost

Rosters of violent dinky Réaumur cribs
exist in interfering pinking tanker gloves
where closures' gristle distances enzyme modules

A mockup or cordage freezes zealous planchettes
hipped settlers sent to shattered Elysian streams
grown pigs or tackling kismet farmers' knuckles puzzle

24 December 1981
New York

24

Baltimore Porches

4

Puzzle pluckers edify weeping peelers
imperiled by banister tricklers' instances
disintegrated telephone fomentations
exaggerate task force dormers' limitless pyramids

Principal glassy clasmatosic purposes
empurple surface ticklers hunger ripples
strips of isotopic temple bumpers pent
in saccharine figurations crucifixes rasp

Rattlers ankle kempt disjunct Wheatenas
physical tinklers clamber from distinctly
though trousered paragon whistlers still resist
inflicted pinhole wipers' artisan wingdings

Singular culmination transfers grasp
at fender tantalizing anise catalysts
simpering pruned defectors rumple swiftly

Swarms of transcendental tergiversations
embolden tonal Campidoglio termites
soon effervescing in strident placental deepeners

24 December 1981
New York

Baltimore Porches

5

Deepeners effectuate disgraceful potage
inane apprentices apportion mootly
as scandalous pachyderms réview escapements
mere fritillaries append to classic nearness

Kinesic desk immobilizers balance quickly
risks finagling artificers argue fragmentarily
airplane soothing candelabras smooth inherently
incoherent thingness Arcadelt aspirations clave

Clever slave enchancing mist propagators
tour enduring fruit ranch crystal bankers' porticoes
roaring spinach flinging passenger titivaters
slit encloistered porcupine chewing praxis distancers

Fists acknowledge the heights of featured panther twisters
mystical particle garterers fend off ferally
jesting of zestful peony hopper dill sop cluers

Gruesome encompassing spoof validifiers
noodle in duty free cloisters or thin tanks
arras deracinators fiber tool kits pierce

26 December 1981
New York

Baltimore Porches

6

Pierce a donkey engine earful gravy meddler
beggars sift or clastic pragmatists flavor
though thoughtfully tossed or tasteless saturators'
safety depredations x out dutiful yang encountered glassworks

Smirking fruit fly exhibiting turnkey critics
fragment clastic figments Yankee polarizers
favor for tankers or encyst unrealistically
prettified pitchblende pentacle horn button tinkerers

Chinks in a chain fence slapstick quivering slave state
liver spot Lincoln bantering cant exhausters
fantasizing fuel enrichment survey pruners
pool in a hagiologically proven Purim blaster

Fast ensnared daredevil thievery figure modelers
prink in a think tank carpet ennobled potion closet
clanking fauxbourdon squealers stink of or sanction

Facets calculate soporific toe warmers
Romeo's messengers masticate Anglo-Saxonly
or trees' enfeebled beer smoke mirrors flippantly

26 December 1981
New York

Baltimore Porches

7

Flippantly the pigeons Portugalize or
perpetrate periphrastic sapience symbolizers
sneaking beside a gun trained guru fork
a Florida hysterectomy panderer lands

Lenses slice or slivovitz interchanges
flatulent bye-byes prideful valerian amplifies
on company time orating orison brokers
plate with passiform pendulum instigation

Mated basic linear diary reform streaks
stick in fixed or frittered pistol dimples
simplified imitation cruisers spook
conducing Zulu Hoovervilles incessantly

Nesting pigs or estivating turtles
lurk in hysterical rhomboid chasmed classrooms
sample screwers fructify or fester away from

Dumb immoderate cluster portion clicketies
snip unfilial vases' pastry faces
limp acknowledged caterpillars frame as crocodiles

26 December 1981
New York

Regular Clerestories

1

Along a network tentacles fended pretense
cleansing autonomous geodes wholly owned
so closely rational graphic entropy
pierced rheostats ensconced in classic creeks

Gears zeroed in on flocculent territories
trenchant teratological fields persisted in
where pinned pacific fertile taskmaster clients
killed coruscating indolent dalliance crusters

Gulled anaesthetic critics cleared directions
though fascinated jumpers gleamed in tandem
and ichthyological centers fended gamely

Granite hooded Greek intolerance tamers
had fated tangents far below the stakes
for grasping clearances or spirited glyphs

Egyptian croziers nosed out portly findings
below inconstant totals sweetly binding

Mean zinc eradicators left out hookups
pellucid fantasists deceived as lookouts

28 December 1981
New York

Regular Clerestories

2

Lookouts claimed or fought for lucid regions
insistent sturgeons fertilized inanely
despite the traffic left on left-hand gleams
and crackers clipped abruptly by thin dreams

Deficient political sticklers hunched in bistros
as fisticuffs calumniated creatures
so widely adolescent filched ensconcements
denounced the crowded calisthenic features

Syrupy dactyls roused no former deserts
unhinged by glib and princely catacombs
though bony partisan tropes sufficed for homes

Heroes of clinical distance dented tents
suffused with rosy lentils dipped serenely
where ghastly zirconium benches floated greenly

Answers hacked in soporific leavings
deceived no trimmers fated for bereavement

Data castanet tanglers tracked a sample
no glistering trees derived as drained or ample

28 December 1981
New York

Regular Clerestories

3

Ample plastic mendacities stick at claques
unhorsed by orisons fostered by slick dogs
while cogs on greasy telescopes frazzle plaques
unmade inlaid or inundated nightly

Syphoned pharmacological tone pump nails
encase strange glassy doorstep penitents
intense enfeebled rotifer palimpsests
enclose as portents panicky lives derail

Sailing closely ennobled three at a time
demoniac sinecure bafflers babble straitly
besmirched by talent or enraged discreetly

Sweating pintos fix perimeter signs
encircled ribosomes belabor curtly
though shallow bearing pockets flock as mutely

Penetrating features sweep kinesic
saturation dramas a planner seizes

Pelagic cryptograms enable steeples
paleontologically crippled

28 December 1981
New York

Regular Clerestories

4

Crippled iodoform spanglers ditch palaestrae
intimate taxidermal cliffs ensorcell
as morsels of hidden practice rack forensic
Dudelsackpfeifers trained by orderly lenses

Strengthened hedonists tackle spiffy Clorox
soggy with driven phantoms parched or cloven
totalitarian sensitizers forage
amid new bantam passenger edifiers

A credible barking tractor pacifier
lances launched encounters soon adroit
between contingent ferned elucidators

Ruined or petulant rampant or ensconced
a crocodilian whisper mirrors fever
embroidering Christian clearances or sweepstakes

Zero effects a grassy paschal notion
as clover integrates a palmy motion

Particulate eons fenestrate depiction
though Alabama bison trick addiction

28 December 1981
New York

Regular Clerestories

5

Addiction liquidates deciduous hormones
a few predicted zeniths flap or sprinkle
assisting critical wrinkles newly bordered
awaiting situational syntheses

Seizures needed by clip joints sickle ink bars
dim felicitated patios glimpse
rewarding labored benthic passion capsules
rapturous sentence farmers actualize

Flimsy lappets pass pristine embankments
cinctured departures verify or mortise
labializing retinated portents

Plosive phagocyte hinderers dampen titles
tampering hexagon torsions simplify
when rooted zebra totals rank immortals

Doors and included segments vent insistent
porticoes or vain topological crystals

Mistier geometric faction blisters
enrich cryonic pantisocratical cisterns

28 December 1981
New York

Regular Clerestories

6

Cisterns vilify checking system access
stigmatizing revelatory trenchers
though hunters' truncheons zigzag practically
relaxing patterns zygotes aspirate

Casual lattices spavin ventral clichés
fine-drawn dancers' firmaments beleaguer
since rinkydink exaggeration plinths
exonerate boracic platyhelminths

Febrile plenipotentiary pokeweed
desists or paginates from A to Z
to fortify lymphatic filter teams

Reams of encrusted lichee tapers prosper
through traumatizing picnics pinned and proper
benignant taxi wardens chill and chop

More dormant crops derive enlightened vines
from agitated phantasmagorical lines

Delighted amplifiers ring a whetstone
divided smartly far beneath a time zone

28 December 1981
New York

Regular Clerestories

7

Time zone annexation savors nest eggs
erected pylon clusters rust complexly
before a roaring torsion borrower flexes
decapitated pigment tallowers' clefts

Eccentric habitant spheres enlist libration
by vibrant nautical sappers' irritation
devaluing centrist episcopal farm oblation
horrific sportsmen apportion ranked and raked

Slaked penetrated axiological clinches
asphyxiate dissipated challenge jigglers
as insincere distracters clamp no inches

Benign deflowering orphans face exactions
Jurassic plenitudes inspire and famish
engirdled lengthily by porphyry factions

Drear synchronies divest tipped tools of richness
when cyclical cavitaters stamp and bitch

Filled anodyne department annelid throngs
are feeding dupes implored to speed along

28 December 1981
New York

42

Megrose Trinity Sixfold

Clasp the crate zone furuncle
negligent pleas designed
devoted though boric twine felt

Melted hysteric rivers bore
terpsichorean thumbprints
buffed photostatic operas

Lavish Javanese hangdog byres
capsulate varnished newsprint
dealt clerical swifts buttress

Rugged princely thermostatic wheezes
ramble in daunted clutches
such as Wordsworth calmed

Morbid pinnacle drinkmarks
signature Brazilian swings
factotums tote bizarrely

Armed inhabitants ventilate
exasperated penetration flasks
on desks arranged as benches clasp

29 December 1981
New York

Filial Simples

Arouse disguised inveterate inner sanctions
close heterophony models rollicking sacredly
where designated ions clamber in hooked felicity

Triumph scares tendentious proxy phantoms
dense rhinoceroses plead against or please
and thieving lithium drillers crisply randomize

Fascinated unctions canvass awkward pitches
where leashes gloss brittle pinnacle trinities
tabulating silent fish vigil print knobs

Notaries coalesce heavestroke neutrality pluck
knuckling cousins' cornerstone rotifers notion-stopping
families blank or bland features tourniquet gauntly

Groins or ghost pickle doers straight-talk furniture
flashes partly important doorstep bin comedies
logarithm wheezes flap or give off

Gusts derive and land by perched nurturer tints
glitter-gauzed Sioux floaters predicate
whenever clam bastion frequency punts arouse

29-31 December 1981
New York

Ten Weeks

Monksday	Mudday	Mustday	Monthday	Mugsday
Jewsday	Duesday	Toothday	Tootsday	Dupesday
Weddinday	Westday	Websday	Wensday	Wetsday
Turdsday	Thirstday	Turpsday	Turksday	Termsday
Fryinday	Frightday	Fightday	Fireday	Vieday
Satireday	Satinday	Sapperday	Sackerday	Sasserday
Sudsday	Someday	Sunkday	Sungday	Sumpday
Mumsday	Mungday	Mushday	Muckday	Muffday
Doomsday	Chooseday	Tombsday	Dudesday	Tubesday
Whenceday	Vexday	Whensday	Wedgeday	Wavesday
Terseday	Sirsday	Turtlesday	Surdsday	Girlsday
Flightday	Vineday	Friarday	Thighday	Flyday
Saggerday	Saddleday	Sanderday	Satyrday	Sadderday
Sonsday	Subday	Sumsday	Suckday	Chumday

"The letters of the week are like the days in the words. . . .
But he could never see that the days performed any useful
function, taken separately. . . . "

from *a. k. a.* by Bob Perelman

1st week: September 1979
Others: January 1982
New York

White Tara

Tires of obstacles
not threat or hit
a setter day object
into it

Intuit onward
song days omitted
splints or fluid wardens
since

Sins decent intervals
intentional multiplication
rationed argosies or murks
stippled faces

Simple phases undeterred
terminal certification
earthdays wry certainties
sickles

Situations thermal grace
furs and foam in classroom
harassment exhibited
dire sovereign

12 January 1982
New York

Sermon Quail

A lost quality simmers. Aquaintance a quaint tense.
Inequality of aptitude. A silence whirrs.
A certainty races idly or towards.

A fortunate dormancy extends heated rushes.
Or look there at the teahouse realities knees.
No deeds there. Unstructured furniture. The furnace.

Certain to turn. Meanings commingle meanings straitly.
Frail straw porch dormers orphans vacate.
Spies. A knifeless turtles day outing. Shouts.

Nouns a pointed cloister interjects. A sacked date.
Offense leverage seasons yellow armatures.
Fleeted reasons a region stencils. A kind stable.

A table cannot conscious. Surface lightness earns a flare.
Scarcity of witness history. A rigged grouping throbs.
Calls. A quiet tubular. A risk insists. Flower walls.

Tall and unnoted thrones estimate. Flavors flake.
A kite's until. Intern and notice. Flow charts crumble.
A crumpled. Security disuse syndromes fuse. Equality.

12 January 1982
New York

Anxious Calm

Wheat and wonted solicitude repeat.
A blight and a report noted tone.
Where phonology destines penance in the offing
Pharaohs desist lest fitters rack.

Sackbuts and unatoned silver clue.
Tools register pardon armatures.

Resist and never soap. Glows fuse.
Notions negate unattained. Frames arm.
Parties clip. Strictures fit list particles.

Strings tincture silent fences.
Dormant corals nested. They fend.

Croziers chrome tackles nightly jar.
Pharmacies parks exited. No one.
Soda mockery fails claim phenomena.
No idea where splits veracity ankles.

12 January 1982
New York

A Lack of Balance But Not Fatal

A motion guided a lotion
in hiding from a tint
reckless from nowhere enforcement.

A label persisted. The past tense
implies it took place. The redness
in which the the implies there was some other
did not persist. He was not waiting long.

The sentence is not always a line
but the stanza is a paragraph.

The whiteness was not enforced.
It was not the other but another
circumstance brought in the waterfall
while a breath waited without being clear
or even happier. A seal was lost without it.

There was a typical edge. The paper tilted
or even curved. A rattle smoothed its way.
Where the predominance stopped was anyone's guess
but the parrot fought for it with forbearance

and a waiting cart was leashed to a trial
though a lie would have done as well
or even better when a moderate sleeve was cast.

No claim was made. A tired park gained.
A lack twisted the bread. Heads foamed.
Nowhere was little enough for the asking.
The task he cleared from the temperature
was outside the extended account. Each the
points to an absence. One or more hiding.

He asked where the inches were. The could have gone.

Intentions are mixed without quotations.
The song was snug. Ambiguity does not
hang in the air. The space between graphemes
is neither colorless nor tasteless. A stream
runs rapidly in no more history. The sweep
of a line. Kindness is not mistaken
for tinder and the lid is resting but shortness
 guarantees no sentence authenticity.

Where the schoolyard was evident a closed
flutter showed a notion without resistant
fences or a paradox without feathers.
Swiftness outlasts the pencil. A cormorant
rose against a born backdrop. Letters inch.
An iconoclast was hesitant. A fire lit.
In the tank a lozenge disengages. Swarms
roared. A special particle felt its form.
Lagging features left oak divination without
a tone or a creased sentinel. Leavings swept.

Toward evening the watchful clock was situated.
No diver called for ether. Lynxes thrived.
Hit by something a silence willed. Streets
were not concerned. A past participle's
sometimes mistaken for a past. An orange
roster was on everybody's mind though clues
could be found. When the ink is incomplete
every table rests on its opposite. A closed
restraint impinged. Furniture rested. Several
pinks in a fist. A clearly charismatic

hideout was read. Neatness wavered. The flag
was wet without exertion or favor. That judge postponed.

Snowfall abused ermines. A folding chair.
Close to the bank a trap was silted though the finder
relaxed without particulars or the least inclination.
Whoever loosed the torrent concluded the tryst.
Finally is the way to find the place. Earshot
is likely. Tones harvest commonplace weather.
The pastness of the past was included in a doctrine
or stakes were wrought. Or sought. Find divers.
Fists rested on the divined peculiarity. Artemis hushed.

Twigs were not grapes. He grasped the talc ring.
Smoothing the horses the clutter died. Finches
sewed roses on the mustered aggregate. Loaves flew.
A mentality ran farther and its crests simmered.
Closeted without bargains the lean rump beheld
no future. A certain flight beckoned. The wonder.
Closed classrooms risk warmth though causation
matters less. Never ink a connection when a plea

is off. Softer dollars were a range without flutters
though a concessive subordinator turns a sentence
into a scene. Dreams were not what he wanted.

16 January 1982
New York

A Variety of Weather

1. Nine Sentences

A variety of weather this winter
was embarrassed at that decision
as a result of that mishap
overnight and over the day Sunday.

That day Sunday variety in this weather
was winterized at that embarrassment
as a decision of that result
over a mishap and overnight.

The night of the day Sunday this variety
was weathered for that winter
as an embarrassment of that decision
over a result and over a mishap.

A mishap of the night this Sunday
varied with that weather
as a winter of that embarrassment
over a decision and over a result.

A result of the mishap this night
Sunday'd with that variety

as a weather of that winter
over an embarrassment and over a decision.

A decision of the result of this mishap
was benighted that Sunday
as a variety of that weather
over a winter and over an embarrassment.

An embarrassment of the decision from this result
mishappened that night
as the day Sunday of that variety
over the weather and over a winter.

A winter of the embarrassment at that decision
resulted from that mishap
as the night of that day Sunday
over a variety and over the weather.

A weather of the winter's embarrassment
decided that result
as a mishap of that night
over the day Sunday and over a variety.

1/24/82 3:06 AM

2. Thirty-Six Sentences

He had seen a variety of Sundays.
He was glad that night of mishaps was over.
The result had long been decided.
He was embarrassed at the winter weather.

The weather came in many varieties.
The day Sunday came before the night.
A mishap resulted.
His decision caused embarrassment all winter.

Winter enjoyed its usual weather.
There are many varieties of Sundays.
Night arrived and a mishap happened.
The result of that decision was embarrassment.

Embarrassment always increases during the winter.
Weather arrived of every variety.
It was day Sunday before it was night.
His mishap resulted from his decision.

His decision led to embarrassment.
It was winter in all ways but weather.
What variety of Sunday was it?
That night a mishap led to a result.

The result was a decision.
He was embarrassed that winter.
The weather was quite varied.
Sunday was the night of the mishap.

The mishap had no result.
His decision caused no one embarrassment.
It was real winter weather.
He had variety that Sunday and that night.

One night there was a mishap.
It was the result of a decision.
It made everybody embarrassed that winter.
We had weather of every variety during the day
      that Sunday.

Was it during the day Sunday or during the night?
A mishap would have been the result.
His decision was embarrassing.
This winter our weather had little variety.

1/24/82 3:33 AM

3. Nine Trios and Twenty-Seven Couples

Variety and weather and winter.
An embarrassment and a decision.
A result and a mishap.
A night and the day Sunday.

Sunday and variety and weather.
Winter and embarrassment.
A decision and a result.
A mishap and a night.

Night and the day Sunday and variety.
Weather and winter.
An embarrassment and a decision.
A result and a mishap.

A mishap and a night and the day Sunday.
Variety and weather.
Winter and embarrassment.
Decision and result.

A result and a mishap and a night.
Sunday and variety.

Weather and winter.
Embarrassment and decision.

A decision and a result and a mishap.
Night and the day Sunday.
Variety and weather.
A winter and an embarrassment.

An embarrassment and a decision and a result.
A mishap and a night.
Sunday and variety.
Weather and winter.

Winter and embarrassment and decision.
A result and a mishap.
Night and Sunday.
Variety and weather.

Weather and winter and embarrassment.
A decision and a result.
A mishap and night.
Sunday and variety.

1/24/82 3:59 AM

4. Thirty-Six Phrases

A variety of Sundays.
A night of mishaps.
A result of decisions.
Embarrassment in winter at weather.

A weather of variety.
One Sunday at night.
A mishap as a result.
A decision through embarrassment in winter.

Winter as to weather.
Variety on Sunday.
The night of the mishap.
The result of a decision without embarrassment.

Embarrassment in the winter.
Weather without variety.
The day Sunday after the night before.
A mishap as a result of a decision.

No decision without embarrassment.
Winter despite the weather.

No variety until Sunday.
A night with a mishap as the result.

Some results of the decision.
No embarrassment because of winter.
That weather with little variety.
Before the day Sunday on the night of the mishap.

Some mishaps in the results.
A decision despite embarrassment.
Winters without any weather.
Variety during the day Sunday but not at night.

One night without mishaps.
No results without decisions.
Less embarrassment in the winter.
Weather of every variety on Sunday.

The day Sunday before the night.
Less a result than a mishap.

Decisions from embarrassment.
No winter without weather of many varieties.

1/25/82 1:05 AM

24-25 January 1982
New York

Hyaline Fixation

Hyaline fixation
models of what is thought
is thinking
and the upshot of the encounter
is not the thought of hyaline fixation
or asphyxiation rapidity
but accurate machines flashing
under fluorescent fixtures
the light always vibrating rapidly
not at all appetizing or rigorous
as what is thought is what is thinking
sufficient for the encounter with the upshot

30 January 1982
New York

This book was set in Garth type at The Writer's Center,
Glen Echo, Maryland. Design consultant was
Kevin Osborn.